Picture the Past
Life on the Trail of Tears

Laura Fischer

Heinemann Library
Chicago, Illinois

© 2003 Heinemann Library
a division of Reed Elsevier Inc.
Chicago, Illinois
Customer Service 888-454-2279
Visit our website at www.heinemannlibrary.com

Produced for Heinemann Library by
  Bender Richardson White.
Editor: Lionel Bender
Designer and Media Conversion: Ben White
Picture Researcher: Cathy Stastny
Production Controller: Kim Richardson

07 06 05 04 03
10 9 8 7 6 5 4 3 2 1

Printed and bound by Lake Book Manufacturing, Inc.

Library of Congress Cataloging-in-Publication Data.
Fischer, Laura, 1977-
   Life on the Trail of Tears / Laura Fischer.
     p. cm. -- (Picture the past)
Summary: Reveals the lives of the Cherokee people who were forced to travel to an Oklahoma reservation in the winter of 1838, discussing their lives before leaving their homes as well as the hardships faced on the trail.
Includes bibliographical references (p.) and index.
  ISBN 1-4034-3800-5 -- ISBN 1-4034-4288-6 (pbk.)
  1. Trail of Tears, 1838--Juvenile literature. 2. Cherokee Indians--Government relations--Juvenile literature.
3. Cherokee Indians--Social conditions--Juvenile literature.
4. Cherokee Indians--Pictorial works--Juvenile literature.
[1. Trail of Tears, 1838. 2. Cherokee Indians--History. 3. Indians of North America--Southern States--History.] I. Title. II. Series.
  E99.C5F57 2003
  973.04'9755--dc21
                                    2003005421

Special thanks to Angela McHaney Brown at Heinemann Library for editorial and design guidance and direction.

Acknowledgments
The producers and publishers are grateful to the following for permission to reproduce copyright material:
Corbis Images: p. 9; Bettmann Archive, pp. 17, 29; Macduff Everton, p. 15; Tim Thompson, p. 22. Dorothy Sullivan/Memory Circle Studio/Norman, Oklahoma, p. 26. Mary Evans Picture Library, p. 24.
Murv Jacob/Tahlequah, Oklahoma, pp. 18–19. National Anthropological Archives/Smithsonian Institution, p. 6. National Museum of the American Indian, p. 28. North Wind Pictures, pp. 8, 30. Peter Newark's North American Pictures, cover and pp. 10, 11, 12, 14, 21, 23. The Bridgeman Art Library: Private Collections, pp. 1, 13.

Illustrations by John James.
Map by Stefan Chabluk.

ABOUT THIS BOOK

This book describes what life was like for the **American Indian** people on the Trail of Tears during 1838 to 1839. The Trail of Tears was a journey the American Indians made when they were forced out of their homeland by the United States **government.**

The trail took the American Indians west to land called Indian Territory. The tribes who walked the Trail of Tears were the Cherokee, Chicksaw, Choctaw, Muscogee Creek, and Seminole. This book focuses on the story of the Cherokee tribe.

The book is illustrated with drawings and paintings from the period and with artists' ideas of how things looked on the trail.

The Author
Laura Fischer is a professional writer and editor residing in Chicago, Illinois. She has worked with a variety of online, magazine, and book publishers, and has a special interest in children's literature and nonfiction. She graduated from Michigan State University with a B.A. in English, and is currently working toward an M.A. in elementary education at DePaul University.

Note to the Reader
Some words are shown in bold, **like this.** You can find out what they mean by looking in the glossary.

CONTENTS

Homeland

For thousands of years, **American Indians** lived in the mountains and forests of the southeastern United States. In the 1800s, **settlers** found gold there. The settlers wanted the American Indians to leave the area. They wanted to start their own communities there. This was the start of a fight over the land. The United States **government** would win the fight, forcing the American Indians out of their homeland. Many American Indians died in their struggle to keep their land.

Look for these
The illustration of a Cherokee boy and girl shows you the subject of each double-page story in the book.

The illustration of a phoenix, a Cherokee symbol, marks boxes with interesting facts about life in the Cherokee Nation.

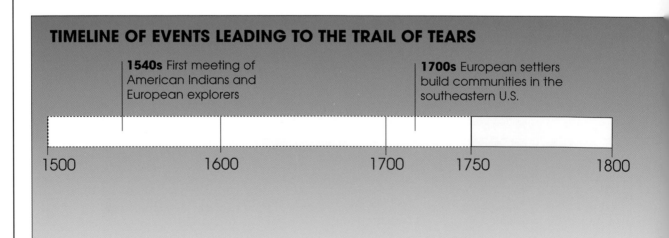

TIMELINE OF EVENTS LEADING TO THE TRAIL OF TEARS

1540s First meeting of American Indians and European explorers

1700s European settlers build communities in the southeastern U.S.

| 1500 | 1600 | 1700 | 1750 | 1800 |

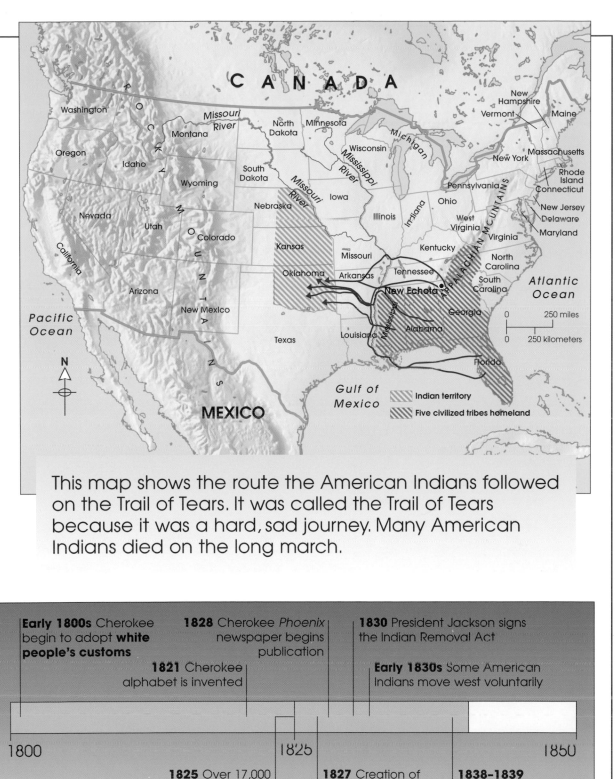

This map shows the route the American Indians followed on the Trail of Tears. It was called the Trail of Tears because it was a hard, sad journey. Many American Indians died on the long march.

Early 1800s Cherokee begin to adopt **white people's customs**

1821 Cherokee alphabet is invented

1825 Over 17,000 Cherokee people live in the southeastern U.S.

1828 Cherokee *Phoenix* newspaper begins publication

1827 Creation of the Cherokee Nation as a constitutional government

1830 President Jackson signs the Indian Removal Act

Early 1830s Some American Indians move west voluntarily

1838–1839 American Indians are forced to move west on the Trail of Tears

1800   1825   1850

Cherokee Life

Around 1830, about 18,000 Cherokee lived east of the Mississippi River. By the 1830s, Cherokees no longer lived in villages. They now had individual farms. Their lives were very similar to those of the white **settlers** around them. **White people** and Cherokees lived in log cabins. Like whites, Cherokees grew corn, wheat, and tobacco on farms, and planted **orchards** of fruit trees.

The Cherokee built log cabins from the trees in the area. A small fireplace heated the cabin and provided fire for cooking food.

In Cherokee towns, people dressed the same as white people and lived in houses similar to those in white areas of southeast United States.

AN ALPHABET

For hundreds of years, the Cherokee language had only a spoken form. Their language had no alphabet, so they could not write it down. In 1821, a Cherokee named Sequoyah created a kind of alphabet, called a syllabary, for the Cherokee language. In this system, each symbol stands for the sound of one syllable. In a very short time, almost every Cherokee learned how to read using this system.

The Cherokee towns had stores where they could buy supplies, and **mills** where flour was made. There were Cherokee schools and a library. Many Cherokee were members of the Christian **religion** and went to church, just as their white neighbors did. But the Cherokee and other local tribes still held on to some of their old **customs.** Some American Indian tribes did not change their ways of life at all.

Whose Land?

For years, little by little, **white people** had been taking over the **American Indians'** land. Now they wanted the rest of the land. The **government** told the Indians to move to an area called Indian **Territory,** 900 miles (1,450 kilometers) west. The government promised them that they would have their own land there. It also promised to pay for their journey and to give them supplies along the way.

INDIAN TERRITORY

The place where the government was sending the American Indians was called Indian Territory. It was in what is today called Oklahoma. At the time of the Trail of Tears, this area had not yet been explored or settled. It was a mostly flat, dry land.

In 1830, President Andrew Jackson signed the law that forced the American Indians from their homeland.

The American Indians did not want to leave their homeland. In 1830, President Andrew Jackson signed a law called the Indian Removal Act. This law said that all Indians must start moving to Indian Territory by May 1838. Now the American Indians did not have a choice. They had to move.

This map of the 1830s shows the states of Georgia and Alabama. This was the main homeland of the Cherokee at that time. The colored areas represent Cherokee and white people's settlements.

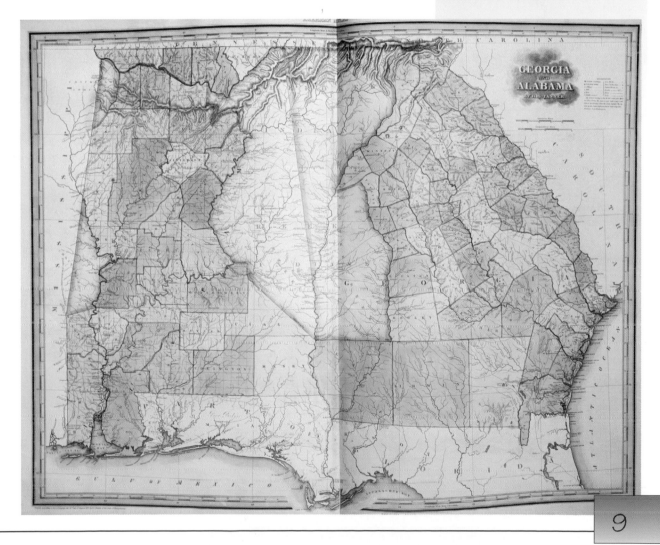

Forced Out

The Cherokee people were divided. Some thought it would be better to leave without arguing than to be forced out. These people packed up their belongings, left their homes, and began moving west to Indian **Territory.** Other Cherokee were angry that they were being told to move. They refused to leave and stayed in their homes.

This picture shows Cherokee **chief** Cunne-Shote. Such chiefs wore traditional Cherokee clothes. The chiefs tried to persuade the U.S. **government** leaders to let them to stay in their homeland.

Chief John Ross led the group of Cherokee who wanted to stay in their homeland and fight the government.

CRUEL TREATMENT

Many Cherokee were rushed out of their homes by the soldiers and treated roughly. They had no time to pack. Sometimes the only things they took with them for the long journey were the clothes they wore. If a soldier did not want to wait for a father or husband to get home from the fields, the group would leave without him and the family would be split up.

Soldiers took these Cherokees from their houses and moved them to **stockades.** The stockades were buildings where the Cherokee would be held before the government sent them on the Trail of Tears. Some were later moved to prison camps because the removal was halted for a while during the summer of 1838 due to a drought.

Thousands of Cherokee were locked up in the **stockades.** Some stockades were so crowded that there was barely room to sit on the floor. The stockades got very dirty and smelly. In the prison camps, many Cherokee became sick, and about 500 died due to illnesses while they waited to start the trip west.

SCARY TIMES

The Cherokee were scared to make a long trip to a place they had never seen. Reports from the time say the Cherokee left the stockades in silence. They may have been thinking about the good lives they were leaving behind.

A portrait of General Winfield Scott, who commanded the soldiers that forcibly removed the Indians from the stockades.

The Cherokee Sequoyah and his alphabet of the tribe's language. By the time of the Trail of Tears, many Cherokee could write down their thoughts and ideas. But on the trail, they could not write their sad story because they had no pens and paper.

Some Cherokee escaped from the soldiers. They fled to the hills of their homeland and hid. But before long the rest of the Cherokee were taken from their homes. Then it was time to start the journey to Indian **Territory.** The Cherokee left the stockades in groups of about 1,000.

The Cherokee traveled about 8 miles (13 kilometers) a day. They started early in the morning and did not stop until evening when they set up camp.

KEEP IN LINE

The first groups of Cherokee to leave each had a white leader called a conductor. His job was to make sure the group followed the right path and stayed on schedule. One group left the stockades every few days.

On the Trail

The Cherokee traveled together on a wide trail through the country. Horse-drawn wagons carried the supplies they would need on the journey, such as food and tools. Young children, sick people, and very old people all rode in the wagons if there was enough room. Everyone else walked next to the wagon that held their supplies. Some traveled by boat, too.

The Cherokee traveled through rain, wind, and cold winter weather. They had tents for shelter and set up camp every night.

Sometimes mothers would ride horses while holding their babies close. Many families, though, did not have horses to ride. Sometimes soldiers rode on horses or walked on foot among the Cherokee. Their job was to keep the Cherokees from trying to run away. They also made sure nobody fell behind.

The trail took the Cherokee through grassland that offered no protection from the weather. Today this land is used for farming and cattle ranching.

The Trail of Tears led to Indian **Territory**— a huge area of grassland, hills, streams, and valleys between the Mississippi River and the Rocky Mountains. The trip to Indian Territory took four to six months. More than 15,000 Cherokees were forced to move. At least 4,000 died on the journey.

At Camp

In the evening, when the sun went down, the groups stopped traveling and set up camp for the night. Every night they unpacked their supplies from the wagons. They searched the wilderness for firewood to build campfires. The men hunted animals, such as rabbits and birds, to eat. Women cooked the evening meal in heavy iron pots over the campfire.

For bedding and covering at night, the Cherokee used the wraps and blankets that kept them warm on the trail. Campfires provided warmth, light, and a way to cook food.

Camp was a time for the Cherokee to look after and feed the horses and **oxen** that traveled with them. Everyone needed to rest after traveling all day. Most people slept on the ground with blankets, but some people slept in the wagons. Some families had tents to protect them from the wind and rain.

NIGHT CAMP

When the trail was first set up, the Cherokee stopped for the night where the soldiers told them to. Sometimes this was on land owned by **settlers.** The settlers would charge the Cherokee a fee to use their land to camp on.

This magazine cartoon of the time shows that some people in the United States did not agree with the harsh way the Cherokee were being treated.

Hard Times

The Cherokee marked their burial places on the trail. When someone died, their family had to keep traveling with the group even though they were very sad.

It was thought that the journey to Indian **Territory** would take three months. Instead it took between four and six months. To begin with, the **government** did not send very many supplies with the Cherokee. What they sent was certainly not enough for even four months. The Cherokee did not have enough food or clothing, and winter had come.

Some Cherokee on the trail had only the summer clothes they wore when they left their homeland. Many more did not have sturdy shoes to wear for walking such a long distance.

The Cherokee were hungry, cold, and tired. So too were their horses and **oxen.** Many people and animals got sick on the journey. Some Cherokee died from illnesses they had caught while being held in the stockades.

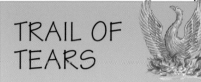

TRAIL OF TEARS

Today we call the Cherokees' journey the Trail of Tears. In the Cherokee language it is called "the trail where they cried."

Getting Supplies

The **government** promised to provide the Cherokee with all the supplies they would need on the trip. This included food, clothing, medicine, and tools. The government hired men to get and deliver the supplies that each group of Cherokee needed. This system did not work well. The men delivered the supplies late, or they did not deliver them at all.

Wagons would often become damaged on the trail, and wagon wheels would break. The tools needed to repair them were scarce.

Rather than starve or abandon their broken wagons, these Cherokee who had enough money sometimes bought supplies from stores and **white settlers** as they traveled on the trail. Many of the white settlers charged very high prices for things. They wanted to make a lot of money from the Cherokee.

On the journey to Indian **Territory,** wealthy Cherokee sometimes stopped at trading posts like this one. There they bought all kinds of supplies and met other **American Indians.**

Children

Cherokee children traveled on the trail with their families. Most mothers and fathers would not let their children out of their sight. They were scared something would happen to them. Sometimes a child walked with an aunt or an uncle. Small children usually rode in wagons. Mothers carried their babies on their backs.

In a modern Cherokee village, a boy makes bows, arrows, and spears. The Cherokee made weapons and tools from pieces of wood and rock, and from animal bones, horns, and antlers.

D Ꭿ Ꮹ Ᏻ Ꭹ

Ꭻ Ꮻ Ꮪ Ꮙ Ꭵ Ꭹ Ꭻ Ꮻ Ꮻ Ꮯ Ꮯ Ꭵ Ꭵ.

CHEROKEE PRIMER.

- PARK HILL:

Mission Press. John Candy, Printer.

Ꭰ Ꮻ Ꭲ Ꭿ Ꮃ Ꮻ Ꮻ Ꭵ: Ꭶ Ꮲ Ꭿ Ꭶ, Ꭻ Ꮪ Ꮲ Ꮻ Ꮻ.
:::::::
1845.

During the day, when they rode in wagons, Cherokee children told each other stories and sang songs. Some may have had reading books, such as this Cherokee book of 1845.

At camp, older boys and girls helped their parents with the chores. They lent a hand with loading and unloading the wagons. They looked for firewood and helped take care of the animals. Sometimes the children played games at camp. Boys would practice shooting arrows at targets on trees. Girls would use rackets to play a game similar to badminton.

NEVER ALONE

Many children had family members who died on the journey. Children whose parents died on the trail were taken in and looked after by relatives or friends.

Clothing

The Cherokee dressed very much like the **white people** of the time. This meant that women and girls wore long skirts or dresses with **petticoats** underneath. They wore long-sleeved blouses and covered their heads with bonnets. Wealthy Cherokee women wore gold jewelry and sometimes placed pins at the necks of their blouses.

A book illustration from the 1800s showing the different kinds of clothing that Cherokee men and women wore.

Cherokee today still make clothing, bags, and shoes in the traditional style, like this shoulder bag. People on the trail would have kept small objects in the bag. The women made the bags from anything they could find or buy on the journey—for example animal skins and fur, and plant fibers.

Men and boys dressed in button-up shirts with vests and wool jackets. They wore long pants and leather boots. Some Cherokee wore the traditional dress of their tribe. Men sometimes wrapped fabric **turbans** around their heads.

Food

When the Cherokee were led by soldiers, they were given a daily **ration** of food that they were allowed to eat. To get more food, the men would hunt and fish at camp. The Cherokee brought food that would not spoil, such as salted meat and dried corn. The women used stones to grind the corn into cornmeal and made porridge, pancakes, and bread with it.

To the Cherokee, corn was a major food source. This illustration shows a Cherokee mother on a corn seed.

The Cherokee sometimes cooked cornmeal on the Trail of Tears. They made it as a simple mush like this one. The mush could be eaten hot or cold. When the mush got cold, it stiffened and could be sliced. The Cherokee would fry the slices of cornmeal mush and serve them hot.

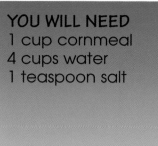

YOU WILL NEED
1 cup cornmeal
4 cups water
1 teaspoon salt

WARNING:

Do not cook anything unless a grown-up helps you. Always let a grown-up do the cooking on a hot stove.

FOLLOW THE STEPS

1. In a medium-sized saucepan, heat the water until it boils.

2. Slowly pour in the cornmeal. Stir the mixture as you pour so it does not form lumps. Add the salt and stir until combined.

3. Cook over high heat for three minutes. Reduce the heat to low, cover, and let the mixture simmer for 20 minutes. Pour the mixture into bowls and serve hot with butter and maple syrup, if you like.

In Indian Territory

When they finally reached Indian **Territory,** the Cherokee people began building a new life. It was not easy because they did not have many of the tools needed to build houses or to plant **crops.** Although it was difficult, the Cherokee slowly got more tools and materials as needed.

Cherokee leaders prepare to meet with Indian Territory **government** officials. Over time the Cherokee people built a strong community like the one they had left behind in their homeland.

The Cherokee who had moved to Indian Territory before the Trail of Tears had already claimed some of the best land for themselves. The Cherokee from the trail settled on land that they were not used to. It was hard and dry. They had to adjust to their new life in a new place.

FAMOUS FIVE

The Cherokee, Chicksaw, Choctaw, Muscogee Creek, and Seminole were known by **settlers** as the Five Civilized Tribes. These tribes, more than any others, followed many **white people's customs.** The settlers believed that these ways of life were the best.

This photograph from the early 1900s shows a Cherokee mother and daughter outside their log cabin Indian Territory.

The Trail Today

Today, the Trail of Tears is a historic landmark. Signs and national parks along the trail tell the story of the Cherokee people who made the painful journey to Indian **Territory.** Museums preserve the culture of the Cherokee people of the southeastern United States. Many groups **re-enact** the sad story of the Trail of Tears so that we will never forget.

According to one legend, the Cherokee rose is a symbol for the Trail of Tears. The white is for the tears shed on the trail. The gold center represents the gold taken from the Cherokee lands. The seven leaves on each stem stand for the seven **clans** that made the journey.

Glossary

American Indians groups, or nations, of people who have lived in North and South America longer than any European settlers

chief leader of a tribe of American Indians

clan group within a tribe

crop plants that are grown in large amounts for using or selling

customs special ways of doing things that have stayed unchanged for many years

government people who make rules for a nation

mill building with equipment to grind grain into flour

orchard group of fruit trees

ox strong animal, similar to a big cow, that is used for work

petticoat thin, lightweight skirt worn under a skirt or dress

ration fixed amount of food allowed daily

re-enact to act out a historical event

religion system of belief in a god, gods, or spirits

settler person who makes a new home in a new place

stockade prison for holding people

territory part of the United States that has not yet become a State.

trade to exchange one thing for another

turban hat made of cloth that is wrapped around the head

white person American whose family originally came from Europe and who has light-colored skin

More Books to Read

Salas, Laura Purdie. *The Trail of Tears, 1838.* Mankato, Minn.: Capstone, 2003

Williams, Suzanne Morgan. *Cherokee Indians.* Chicago: Heinemann Library, 2003.

An older reader can help you with this book:

Burgan, Michael. *The Trail of Tears.* Minneapolis: Compass Point Books, 2001.

Index